Charles Heathcote has alw
very rarely leaves. He is the
northern comedy novels a
and her schemes. His pc
Butcher's Dog, and t
Cloudbursts, and Landscapes
Shepherd's Delight is his first poetry collection.

Shepherd's Delight
Charles Heathcote

VA
Various Altitudes
Cheshire

Longclough was previously published in Landscapes (Empress Publishing, 2018)

Woolgathering was previously published in the 12th edition of Butcher's Dog Magazine, 2019

The Barefoot Roamer was previously published in the "Transform" edition of The Greenhouse Magazine, 2023

Mary had a little lamb
with peas and roast potatoes.
It hadn't known when it was born
to love her would be fatal.

Ovine Gynaecology

The ewe has its reed out.

Dad says to press the hot mass of pink flesh back inside.
My fingers squelch against the steaming conical,
force each fold of rigid flesh into the sheep's darkness.
Dizzy from bending down for so long,
I wonder when I will get to wash my hands or
if lunch will be eaten with the worry of e-coli.

Dad stitches a truss to her back end:
both farmer and physician
yet still she complains –
bleats and heaves herself
as though we've inconvenienced her,

this cold April morning

where the white balance is off and sheep hide in bushes,
birth lambs with crowns of gorse,
and all sound leaves the world save for lowing and
cackles.

This is the real beauty of spring:
the sheep rule this empire, where
crows bide their time as lambs frolic

a clan of wool, trailing prolapses
that it is our penance to fix.

sheep die

they go lame, don't eat, don't drink,
don't take to antibiotics, store
rotting lambs inside them for Dad
to pull out bit by bit: skull, leg,
kidneys, toes, a jigsaw puzzle,

build your own livestock

then the lambs who live break their ribs,
suffocate themselves in the spring heat;
a feast for buzzards and crows
and badgers and foxes

the ewes with milk fever will not be saved
and ramblers won't put their dogs on leads,
there's too much grass then it's not enough,
there's torrential rain, worry of drought,

the ewes become stressed, the lambs follow suit
the tups go crazy in the field

Lambs

We drag them from the womb,
revel in the sound of lambs blarting,
spend hours admiring the fullness of their bellies,
the swell of mother's milk.

We bring home cade lambs
the sick, the orphaned, the odd triplets,
bottle-feed and cradle them, grow attached but

come October, we will pack them into trailers,
traverse the country for the best price,
argue with auctioneers over catalogue placement.

We value lambs' lives more than the butcher;
each bleat silenced puts clothes on our backs,
food on the table, pays our rent.

The Barefoot Roamer

He hasn't worn shoes since the seventies
after dancing on his wedding day
resulted in blisters the size of pennies
and the bride running off with a
bus driver from Milton Keynes.

He claims that his toes appreciate the freedom to wiggle
to feel the heat of sun-drenched gravel;
has been known to tie them together with daisy chains.

His soles have hardened like granite
from traipsing throughout Cheshire, ignorant
to all the muck in farmer's fields.
He's squelched through owl pellets and cow pats,
stepped in badger latrines and fox scat,
simply laughs it off and calls it moisturising.

Yet when he's alone of an evening,
soaking the day from between his toes,
he wonders what it would be like
to have someone take his heels in their hands
wipe away the dirt, caress away the aches,
and wander with him barefoot through the world.

An Education in the Attitudes of a Sheep Farmer

Don's a farmer whose face is crags,
mountainous. He serves
home-made lemonade, chats to Dad.

I pull my sleeves over my hands,
burrow into my jumper, lost
amongst the threads, the seams,
the scent of detergent and wet dog.

I cannot speak to this man. I don't know how:
my tongue is dead in my mouth
like a slug drowned in salt.

Dad jokes, hides serious talk behind swear words –
twelve more lambs dead, more sheep lame,
their condition made worse by rain.

This is how men should behave,
all humour, bravado.

A man who wants to be a farmer
needs confidence and a loose tongue
and I've neither.

I am not built for this,
should have stayed home

yet I remain in this cold farm cottage

like a badger in a hedgerow, undeterred.

Fantastic Mr.

I like the idea of the fox.
A trickster, a devil, our very
own Loki, certainly low-key
as he sneaks into the field,
finds his way through gorse,
brambles, you name it. He has
a plan for this heist. The
Danny Ocean of the countryside.
He steals lambs, prefers the
weak ones, those that don't struggle,
make it easy. Once, maybe
he is starving, maybe he watches us
and thinks he'll have a go, give
the ewe a hand, help her birth
the lamb; uses his teeth,
develops a taste for fresh meat.
The mother is left for dead.

The fox is found two days later,
doesn't escape the bullet.

The Rainbow Farmer

erects a Pride flag beside his scarecrow,
sings along to Orville Peck
as he drives his New Holland through Rainow.

He stops to chat with the Pickfords,
they need a wall building
and wonder if the wrists of a gay farmer
are strong enough for the job.

He doesn't challenge them to an arm wrestle,
has learned not to embarrass a man in front of his wife;
hair zebra-striped, tell-tale signs of a home dye gone awry.
He recalls being fifteen and fancying Robert Sugden,
airing his attraction subliminally, with frosted tips,
and loosening more buttons on his school shirt.

He'll catch the wife at karaoke on Friday,
buy her a vodka and watch her
caterwaul her way through *Hungry Eyes.*
She'll invite him to theirs for a Sunday roast,
in thanks for mending their drystone wall,
say that he can bring a "friend" if he likes.

He won't tell of the men who leave his bed,
do not care for rural life, or cows who stare in judgement
when they roam the countryside.

He has his Pride flag beside his scarecrow
who wears a checked Hollister shirt
that once belonged to an ex-boyfriend
who didn't care for dirt.

Briefing for a Descent into Vegetarianism

It begins with a burger –

prime beef clenched between teeth,
fat pooling on my taste buds,
marinates, blends flavours

only as I chew do I second guess my choice.

My uvula becomes a boulder
I cannot swallow
    what if I am eating somebodies' mother?

The sesame seed bun is a coffin,
the lettuce and tomato a shroud
gherkins like formaldehyde,
drowned
under a special sauce
and cheese like cellophane

because,

this burger is a corpse:
the ground-up remains of an Aberdeen Angus
offered up to assuage my gluttony

with each bite I wonder if the cow lived well
before
    the bolt to the brain
    the metal rod rammed into the skull and spun –
quickly kill the nerves –
    like Ancient Egyptian excerebation

then, the butchery: skinning
            boning
            carving
the grinding

or

if theirs was a life of misery
until its inevitable end.

Not one to waste food, I devour the burger,
warts and all, corpse and all,
a small subsection of cow is all
that slithers down my gullet,
lays heavy in my gut.

My body is a graveyard, a mausoleum,
a tomb.

Mrs. Hoggett's Career Move

Officially, she performs burlesque,
struts on stage, untying her apron strings
as the audience caterwaul.

She sashays to the songs of The Wurzels,
slowly slips from her wellington boots while
they make promises of combine harvesters,
arches her toes with their fresh pedicure –
nail polish red as pig's blood.

Apron's removed to reveal pheasant feathers
covering her unmentionables.
There are wolf whistles
and she grins,
proud that she was never ticklish.

She sways beneath the stage lights,
purses her lips as seductively
as any sow over a boar and
gently, tentatively
reaches for her left breast –

she has been lambing sheep for years,
she knows how to build anticipation –

she discards the feathers one by one
unveils her pierced nipples
each adorned with a lucky rabbit's foot.

The song builds to a crescendo
and the audience are over-eager.

She reaches below her belly button
tears away the final feathers and twirls,
swings her hips from left to right,
bounces the fox tail that hides her behind.

Once the music ends, and the lights dim,
the crowds go home and she's alone
with a photograph of the farm she longs to save,
she dreams of when she can do it again.

Family History

Well, the farmer begat a farmer
and then he had a butcher
and butchery proved the better trade
when his brother begat a farmer
he took him on as a butcher
but the farmer's son didn't care for butchery.
The farmer's son gave a fortnight,
crashed his bike and he scarpered
said as farmers are not made for butchery –
he went off to become a shepherd,
a disappointment to his parents
who thought cows far superior to sheep.

On Saturday Afternoons

Cowboys rule the living room.

I treat the arm of the settee like a Mustang,
mimic the men on horseback as they
fire pistols at the ululating enemy.

I wonder why the Power Rangers don't step in,
their colourful spandex adorned with fringe and
spurs on their Megazords.

Dad drinks tea from a stained pint mug,
pays little attention as my brother
Andrew hovers behind the curtains
continues his endless game of hide and seek.

All the while, I anticipate the singing,
brace myself to hear *rolling*,
rolling, rolling, raring to ride along
and roar *Rawhide!*

Inventory

He has palatial pockets,
checks them before he leaves:
phone, wallet, keys,
bale string and Heptavac P
nuts, bolts, and a toffee hammer
fag ends and humbug wrappers.
Ancient condom, lambing snare,
rotten remains of a mouldy pear.
Shoelaces and sunflower seeds,
spade-shaped truss for sheep's prolapsed reed.
Wife's knickers that he found up his sleeve –
he'll return them when he feels the need.
Sellotape and chewing gum,
used gun cartridges, paracetamol.
Teabags, teaspoon, rusty syringe,
Voltarol for when his hips twinge.
Toilet paper, nasal spray,
penknife to unwrap bales of hay.
Dog biscuits, beet pulp, sachets of salt
no vinegar 'cause he can't handle malt.
He has an acorn, a conker and a rabbit's foot
and his pockets are insulated with bits of straw and wool,
and it might seem a lot, but this is no magic trick;
he has left no room for his cheese sandwiches.

Numeracy Lessons, 1964

He learns to count at Longclough,
drowning kittens in a water bowser -
a favour to his mother. 'If there
are any cats left in the yard when
I get home, you're in for a clout.'

He hangs them on the clothesline
dripping onto the drystone. The dogs
worry at the brittle kitten carcasses.

His Mum returns on the Wincle bus,
says she was only messing.

In the Bottom Field

Barely daybreak, reading Steinbeck
in the Land Rover passenger seat –
playing the waiting game. All Biblical;
a shepherd watching sheep.

No sign of foxes or badgers.

A lamb's only threat is the magpie,
hidden in the hedgerows,
squawking murder like a phlegmatic grandmother.

I've hours ahead with little to do but
observe dew steam as the world awakes,
listen to the lowing of sheep,

their obnoxious bleats.

Midmorning, I eat half my lunch –
break up the day –
attempt to ascend a hill too steep
for men to climb, just because.

Rehabilitation

Mildred is brought home to die,
new-born, spine severed.

We prescribe a quiet death,
mix a concoction of painkillers,
brandy and milk –
watch her drift into a dreamless sleep.

Next morning,
we wake to bleating.

Why Nana Alice Left £90,000 to Donkeys in her Will

She remembers trips to Blackpool
as a girl, though she can't recall
who took her, parcelled off to
family like Uncle Albert in Fools
and Horses.
    it was a different world, fish and
    chips on the front, Jeye's Fluid and
    donkey muck left to stink in the
    thick heat.
She adores donkeys –
their maudlin faces, the bows in
their tails and the way
their fur bristles to the touch.
    could spend all day riding back
    and forth through the throngs of
    folk in their bathing costumes –
    they the Israelites and she the
    Queen of Sheba.

Years later,
    married, with four children
    gambolling about the farm
    like feral cats,
she brings the donkeys in.
There isn't much work off-season,
and she has fields free. With any luck
they'll hit the nobhead indoors
where it hurts.
    when the donkeys leave their trailers
    they are calm, cowed, patient.
    The moment their harnesses come off
    they are wild.
She watches from behind a drystone wall,
her tears spit into her hair, blown by
a biting wind she's only known at Longclough.
    the donkeys are free to play
    like schoolboys with marbles,
    too soon they will leave
    and she can't go with them.

Carnivore

I eat corpses on a daily basis.

Fry ground up cow
add cheese,
squeeze between buns.

Masticate, really mull over
the taste of fear and fat.

There's grilled pig for breakfast,
sliced thick and cooked till crisp,
just like eating your grandmother.

On Sundays we make a real meal of things
cook an entire bird, toss out the bones.

One day we will forego the butcher,
head straight for the morgue
help mourners save money on cremations.

The Latest from my Nephew

No, Mrs Spiller,
I don't need to read and write.
I'm not going to be a writer,
I'm going to be a farmer.

He is the opposite of me,
loud, gregarious, will play
in mud, a piglet having fun.

He loves the chickens I call devils
holds them to his chest, buries his
face in the feathers on their necks.

There is no silence about him,
no whispers or whimpers,
murmurs or sighs.

He is all bangs and roars
a firework in child form.

Marooned

They've tarmacked the drive where
we once squelched through mud
that wrapped around our knees,
held tight as we struggled to lift our feet.
Wellington-booted, weighed down
waiting for Dad to heft us out,
ferry us to a shore of stone.

He saved the youngest first.
I, the eldest, stuck fast
concreted in almost. Toes fixed, twitched
as a chill wind taunted me
whispered down my neck that I would never be free.

Meanwhile, Dad ambled to save us, one by one,
tested the elastic of time.

When my turn arrived,
he heaved; hands dug beneath my armpits
but the mud held firm.
I was bogged.

Dad dragged me upwards.
My feet birthed from my wellies
and I clung tight, like a shipwrecked passenger to a
wardrobe door.
The chill wind bit my ankles, threatened next time.

I wonder if they salvaged my wellies before laying the
drive,
or if firm rubber stands immured beneath the tarmac.

Shepherd's Delight

He's barely seventeen,
got a new licence in his pocket,
sweaty palms on the steering wheel
of the clapped-out Land Rover
he's borrowed from his father.

There's a stink of haylage and wet dog
that he's tried to cover up with
Lynx Dark Temptation, but he
swears the stench still lingers

and he wonders what she's thinking
in the passenger seat, dressed
for a trip to the cinema. Instead,
they're at the top of Blaze Hill,
stargazing, waiting for the sun to rise.

She makes the first move, unfurls
his hands – teaches him to steer.

Hideout

It smells green beneath the trees:
wet grass   sheep muck.
The scent of countryside nostalgia.

There is an air of quiet. A thin stream
burbles like a calmed infant as the
harsh terror of winter seeps

into the earth.

Mud

ankle deep. I'm grateful for my cracked wellies
though they're two sizes too big and I can't bend my legs,
trapped in a mossy rubber prison.

This is my moment of peace before the onslaught
of sheep arrive, storm up the field

two-hundred filthy clouds:
a Spring-time hurricane.

Cuckoo

It is the gradual depression of shoulders as
his son chooses action figures over Tonka trucks;
die-cast tractors gather dust at the base of the toybox,
(neither lost nor misplaced simply forgotten)

and there is a long sigh when the growing lad
still cries too much in the playground.
He doesn't hold with sticks and stones,
tries to solve problems with words,
can't make sense of the world.

He has weary resignation and mournful eyes when
his son shows no interest in sheep or girls,
tractors or farming or auctions or Westerns,
disregards wellies and waterproofs,
bale string and wall building.

Son prefers home comforts, cannot abide mud,
rolls his eyes and shakes his head
when he sees Dad arrive home caked in filth
from bobble hat to rubber soles
and leaves his wellies by the back door.

Hayfever

He puts the fox out of its misery;
a bullet to the skull silence

had been ploughing the field
unsuspecting, unaware, until

high-pitched keen,
bellow, wail

merciless mewling tearing through the quiet
     and a mangled fox,
     back legs torn off,
     shredded.
     Gelatinous clods of blood and tissue
     left for the crows to pick at,
     sheep to sample.

It tried to drag itself away,
still sure it would survive
as nothing more than torso.

When he tells me what he has done
I wonder at this man; my brother
the child who threw cups during
hide and seek
     split lip, iron taste
     laughter sharp as tin

how he always had a wildness
        wandered around the house
        naked and feral
                refused offers of
        underwear and socks.

His clothes were a prison.

He longs for days outside
acquiring filth
        badges of honour
        pockets filled with hay,
        straw, bale string.

Sees the world in black and white;
once took a pocket knife to school
to kill a lad who wronged him.

Perhaps it's too much time spent around dogs
        had worms at six
        brought home fleas
        will drop his trousers and piss
        whenever he feels the need.

He's always had the hunter inside
wishes to sample human flesh
just to know the taste,
questions if we're all pigs
who managed to escape

      shoots pigeons and crows
      moles and badgers
and now this fox
      scrabbles across the ploughed field
      beribboned intestines trail behind her.

He raises the gun,
calls it mercy.

At the Abattoir

Chickens hang from hooks
machine-plucked, still twitch
post-electrocution.

Costs

There used to be a farm here, now it's a B&B
a dozen gypsy caravans though that isn't quite PC
they let them out to city dwellers and the odd townie
who are easily pleased with WiFi and glitchy Sky TV.

(and can't tell the difference between a cow and a sheep)

You want the countryside without the farmers,
the doting faces of calves without the cows;
don't want to be reminded of last night's beef burger
as you listen to their lowing and their moans.

You want to ramble down a public footpath
without the worry of stepping in sheep muck.
Lambs are fine for springtime, get them gone by summer
you don't want them impinging on your view.

I've no issue with development, but this just isn't it.

There used to be a farm here, now it's a B&B.
Folk used to come for miles to sample their delicacies;
from jam and marmalade to red onion chutney
there's no more tasting preserves now it's a B&B.

(still can't tell the difference between a cow and a sheep)

You say they've ploughed the fields, it's time to scatter,
leave farming to the supermarkets and turn
the countryside into a family attraction
with fewer bovines and more Portaloos.

You want to turn the fields into a retail development:
cull the cows, make way for Burger King,
don't need fresh air if you've got a bowling alley
a cinema and a 24-hour gym.

(I could blame big business, but this is your fault.)

There used to be a farm here now it's a B&B.
The cost became too much and nothing is ever free
so the farmer let the fields and sold his machinery
but it wasn't enough, now his farm's a B&B.

(I won't say what happened to the cows and the sheep.)

Views from the Top of Beard's Hill

I

From the top of Beard's Hill, see White Nancy;
recall thinking it a shed, a large shed
certainly the biggest of all the sheds
but a shed nonetheless.

II

See Don's from the top of Beard's Hill,
though he's been dead twelve years
it's still his cottage, his field.

They've tarmacked the drive
so as not to ruin their pick-up's paintwork
Dad says, *I don't know why you'd buy a
pickup you didn't want dirtied.*

III

Dad runs dogs at the top of Beard's Hill,
trains them on shearlings in the round pen,
keeps a Tesco carrier tied to a stick
for when they grab hold, all teeth and wool.

IV

Feel King of the World at the top of Beard's Hill,
strut around like a cockerel,
twirl a drainpipe like a sceptre.
There is no fear here, no war councils with the mind,
these are days of warm lemonade and ants crawling into
your socks.

Pollution as a Form of Population Control

Let's build on green belt land,
tarmac the countryside. Get rid
of farmers, and, when the air
becomes unbreathable   little more than smog

we'll fund unaffordable housing,
pack the common in like cattle

watch them fight for survival

they won't last long   leave more space

to knock it all down, start again,
build a golf course in its place.

Too Bleak for TV

How do you feel? asks the man from the news.

Dad doesn't answer immediately,
can't thump a television presenter.

He stares at:

the heap
                        the heavy mound of burning corpses
his entire crew
                                    his workforce
those he could moan about Mum to

                    are dead

there will be compensation
                            the government say
the farmers don't care either way
                                the activists say
they only cry over the money
                                    lost

How do you think I feel? Dad asks.

There's a Power Ranger at the top of Beard's Hill

He flies down a drainpipe to fight Astronema's monster,
but doesn't make it out the other side. I peek into
the darkness and see nothing but the grass beneath me.

Dad can't find him either, says as the drainpipe
must be a portal to another world, that the black ranger
goes where he is needed most.

I keep up the search, circuit the fields, wander
from muck midden to dog shed and back –
question how the team will go on missing a member

who will protect Angel Grove?

Dad says as he didn't have toys growing up. His presents
were pencils and colouring books. I bet the drainpipe
portal took the black ranger to him

maybe protecting sheep in Rainow will help save the
universe.

What it Means to be a Man

Dad skins two rabbits in the kitchen sink,
tears their bodies with his bare hands;
livers squashed between thumb and forefinger,
the heart left to spin down the plughole.

Bones crack and squelch,
seep against fake stainless steel
simmer in the sunlight.

He fries the rabbits in butter,
feeds them to our Mark,
whose teeth snag on hair and fur
and I laugh because he cannot stomach the job,

can't hold himself with
the resigned determination of a man -
all steely eyes and clenched jaw.

I'd have eaten the head first,
proved to Dad I am capable;

I am not the tears in the playground
and the fear of the dark,
can take the threat of a belt without an asthma attack

but fathers make mice of
mountains of men, pounce
like cats beneath cupboards

unearthing secrets
can wrench apart their son's ribcage with a look.

Child's Play

Flora rediscovers her youth in the back garden

like a pup, she whips
the small furless ball into the air
watches it fall
snatches it between her teeth

competes with gravity

shakes the lump from side to side and back again;
a toddler playing at ragdolls in the grass
the dirt.

This is no game

the cat is not frantic at the sight of the dog
but what she holds between her teeth,

this small pouch of a thing, barely leather,
eyes unopened, mewls unheard.

We bury Flora's plaything beside the daffodils,
cover the grave with rocks.

Grinagog

I never saw you smile, although I
knew your mischievous smirk –
the one you used at the bakery
when you bulk-ordered lemon buns
after a visit to the diabetes clinic.

I recall the glee you found in sugar;
adding it by the basinful to your tea –
remaining unfulfilled.

You were always mauve, kept your
shoulders down, eyes on the pavement,
scurried through town, hoping to get hit by a bus.

Perhaps I did see your smile,
but never noticed.

You didn't catapult through days;
a thrill-seeking adventurer, grinning
with the adrenaline of it all.
You were content with small pleasures,
found delight in the simplicity of a lemon bun.

The Butcher's Boy

The butcher's boy rides his bicycle through Bollington,
he brings cuts of meat in brown paper packages
knocks at the door of Mrs Hollinshead,
she has a craving for proper pork sausages.

The butcher's boy rides his bicycle through Bollington,
not that he wants to, but it pays good wages.
He wants to roam wild moors, shepherd sheep,
to comb the woods alongside his collie.

The butcher's boy is tossed from his bicycle in
Bollington,
when a tractor passes and knocks him into a verge.
He has scrapes on his hands, smashes his collar bone,
and the driver just laughs as he heads back to the hills.

The boy brings his bicycle back to the butcher,
scowls his way past a queue of mad customers,
tells the butcher to sod his black pudding and
keep the bike. He can deliver his own pissing tripe.

To the Rescue

Snowdrifts blown six-feet-high block
the fences, the gates, the drystone walls.
Colourless sky, skeletal white
full of sadness and broken promises.

A fearless farmer drives down Blaze Hill,
his Land Rover wheezes as the farmer disregards
the threat of black ice on tarmac,
groans to a halt – the handbrake
stiff and unyielding.

The driver's door clatters against the road,
followed by the exhausted anger of a
farmer who has known worse winters.

He reattaches the door with bale string,
a trusted friend, and eyes
the mess the wind has made.

His sheep bleat within their
frozen prison. His femurs fix to ice as
he recognises the job at hand.

He tosses a sack of beet pulp across his back,
begins the trek to find his sheep. He heaves
a breath,

climbs into the snow.

since you became my dead grandmother

you've transformed into a myth –
mystical as mist, Narcissus in his river

your hallucinations are no longer
the meanderings of a mind mithered by a UTI,
vascular dementia, or the product of age;
they are portents of doom, visions of the future,
premonitions from an ancient Oracle

your temper is now a rage fit for Hera;
that tendency to impale your children
with a poker through their thighs
is a fable – a cautionary tale –
Achilles and his ankle

your lemon buns have become ambrosia,
James Herriot: idolatry.

you've transformed into a legend –
a daughter of Mnemosyne.

Longclough

We drive up the Cat and Fiddle to a
stone farm track the old fella won't tarmac
so that the Land Rover jolts, clatters, sprays
pebbles at the paintwork. We cross
the fields, grass as pale as ashes, thin
black reeds grope from beneath the earth,
damned demons pleading for salvation;
reaching towards a sky full of clouds, mist white,
where buzzards dance with crows, fight
with gulls for dominance, for the
slim pickings of a fresh dead lamb.
Moles poke fun at us, poke noses from their hills,
the ultimate kamikaze mission – if the birds
don't get them, Dad will – and rabbits
dig their holes beside badger setts, their
pockmarks and craters are acne scars upon
this prehistoric skin. A chimney smokes up ahead,
perhaps Nana Alice is burning a tree again,
its trunk filling the living room. There are no fire
hazards in Macclesfield Forest. We reach
the swamp, a farm yard of knee deep mud, where
old cars go to die, their parts Frankensteined
onto other faulty machines. The thick stench of
cow muck crams itself down our throats as we
enter the shippon – the last leg of this quest –
through darkness, where the shadows of old
equipment spread fear, pace quickens at the
sight of a scythe. Strange to think that I will
no longer make this journey, that the farm is not ours,
it's somebody else's dream up in flames.

A Northumbrian Winter

Piss wet through piss wet through
coat and trousers piss wet through
Mummy, Daddy, Frank and Harry
in my drawers and in my wellies
no idea what we'll do
we're piss wet through with snow.

- from the poet's nephew, aged four

Went to try and corn the sheep
couldn't find them for the sleet
lost the feeling in my feet
piss wet through with snow.

Tried the quad and 4x4
couldn't get them up the moor
feet were really getting sore
piss wet through with snow.

Took a spade, took a shovel
to clear the road at the double
the pay is barely worth the trouble
still piss wet through with snow.

If you think you've had it tough,
I don't bluster, I don't bluff.
Northumberland is bloody rough
it's piss wet through with snow.

Murder of Crows

If he can kill every crow in the world
he will, has held a grudge
since he walked into a field
and saw the purple-plumed predator
slurping a lamb's intestines like spaghetti.
    They'd already had its eyes
        pecked clean from its two-day old skull,
    its legs spread-eagled
woollen twigs spattered with blood
from the open cavity of its stomach.

Now, not a single corvid is safe.

Magpies are forever sorrowful
shot with enough force
it's as though they never existed

disintegrated

black and white and red all over.

He catches a jackdaw
pins it to a wall and listens to it squawk

fixes it with a glare filled with memory
and twists its head from its neck

easier than popping the lid off a tube of Pringles.

Numeracy Lessons, 2002

I am no good at counting sheep.

We take the Land Rover around the fields –
Dad's eyes shrewd, quick as Mr Miyagi after that fly,
as he does his sums – calculates –
here a Gritstone, there a Herdwick
with the occasional Jacob because of Andrew's
proclivities.

Soon enough,
they're counted up.

Dad has his fifty-six while I lost count at seventy-eight.

I am no good at counting sheep.

Standoff

The blue bull pays no attention to fences,
barks steam from his nostrils glowers at me

fearsome as the night Dad was eaten by an alligator.

I hope this goes the same way;
it's all a pile of sheets,
my over-active imagination,
the nightmare of a four-year-old gone to bed on
Crocodile Dundee.

I remain stock still,
eye to eye with the bull.

A standoff reminiscent of Dad's Westerns:
Gunfight at the OK Corral, The Good, the Bad,
and the Ugly, A Fistful of Dollars, True Grit.

I am alone.
My only defence a cowardly border collie.

Dad's sharp whistle cuts the air.
The bull, disinterested, moves on.

Bury me in my Wellies

I've had this pain in my side for a while
that twists my guts like twine.
I planned to see the doctor,
but I couldn't find the time.
I'd sheep in need of worming,
foot-rotting, that sort of thing
I could've asked my son
but he's got no time for farming.

Well now it's two in the morning
and my side it don't half hurt
like I've just been gored by a Jacob's horn
and it's torn right through my shirt.
I've called the paramedics,
they say they're on their way
but if they don't get here in time,
I've just one thing to say:

Bury me in my wellies
they're all I've ever known
and if there is an afterlife
I want to feel at home.
There's souls that need a shepherd
and they will flock to me so
bury me in my wellies
beneath the old yew tree.

The pain isn't going anywhere,
but I've made it down the stairs
hopefully no one minds
finding me in my underwear.
I'll put on my coat and wellies
and switch on the porch light;
if it's my time for dying
then I'm going to do it right.

Well the paramedics are here in ten,
and they're prodding me like I'm Play-Doh
asking questions, attaching machines as
my son arrives for the floorshow.
He's by my side with his fretting,
he's worried and he's stressed
so I take his hand in mine
and make my final request:

Bury me in my wellies
they're all I've ever known
and if there is an afterlife
I want to feel at home.
There's souls that need a shepherd
and they will flock to me so
bury me in my wellies
beneath the old yew tree.

I'm in the ambulance in quick-sticks
and rushed down to A&E
they're saying it's an hiatus hernia
which I thought was a fallacy.
They take me off to theatre
with no time for a brew
gone like a shot, out like a light,
before I could refuse.

I open my eyes to bright white
and my side still aches a bit,
that's supposed to go away in Heaven
so I guess I must have lived.
My son, he sits across from me
as concerned as his mother
who passed over twenty years ago.
I thought I was off to meet her.

Still, my time it isn't far away
and when it comes, I ask that you

Bury me in my wellies
they're all I've ever known
and if there is an afterlife
I want to feel at home.
There's souls that need a shepherd
and they will flock to me so
bury me in my wellies
beneath the old yew tree.

Woolgathering

Dad sets a task to search the fields for wool,
locate all the stray pieces
pack them into hessian sacks.

The hard part is done, he says,

his callused hands think nothing of gorse,
or barbed wire,
anywhere the stray white frays get caught.

I set out.

I pick through sheep muck and thick mud
for mere wisps of wool,
memories of wool,
shreds, the dregs,
barely feathers of wool

press them amongst the full coats,
feel the wax of lanolin.

Acknowledgements

I wish to express my utmost gratitude to Joy Winkler who encouraged me to explore poetry and has provided much support and guidance. Thanks also for starting Poems and Pints at The Button Warehouse, where I got to test drive a lot of the poems featured in this collection.

My family and our exploits were a great source of inspiration so thank you to them. A special mention to Cathryn Heathcote for accompanying me to a great number of events over the years.

Thank you to the early readers of this collection, Charlie Brook, Emily Novelle and Ann Platt.

It would be remiss of me not to acknowledge Phil Poyser, who said that I ought to call myself a poet. Indeed, thank you to The Macclesfield Creative Writing Group for reading and critiquing my work.

Thanks also to the editors who thought a handful of these poems were suitable for publication in their magazines.

To those who have been here since the beginning, until next time, that is all.